love,
John

Age Before Beauty

Compiled by
Rita Freedman

PETER PAUPER PRESS, INC.
WHITE PLAINS · NEW YORK

*For Gloria, Sharon and Evie—
ageless beauties!*

Copyright © 1991
Peter Pauper Press, Inc.
202 Mamaroneck Avenue
White Plains, New York 10601
ISBN 0-88088-727-3
Printed in Hong Kong
7 6 5 4 3 2

AGE BEFORE BEAUTY

Why not fall in love with the body you've been sleeping with all your life?

Stewart Emery

The average man is more interested in a woman who is interested in him than he is in a woman—any woman—with beautiful legs.

Marlene Dietrich

Youth is a disease from which
we all recover.

Dorothy Fuldheim

If Jack's in love, he's no judge
of Jill's beauty.

Benjamin Franklin

When you're twenty and
pretty, then you're rather like
Switzerland—beautiful
but dull.

Faye Dunaway

What a strange illusion it is
to suppose that beauty is
goodness.

Leo Tolstoy

It's sad to grow old, but nice to ripen.

Brigitte Bardot

Beauty is all very well at first sight; but who ever looks at it when it has been in the house three days?

George Bernard Shaw,
Man and Superman

The hardest years in life are those between ten and seventy.

Helen Hayes,
at age eighty-three

The great thing about being 30 is that there are a great deal more available women. The young ones look younger and the old ones don't look nearly as old.

Glenn Frey

She may very well pass for
   forty-three
In the dusk with a light
   behind her!

W. S. Gilbert,
Trial by Jury

Your body is just like a bar of
soap. It gradually wears down,
from repeated use.

Ritchie Allen

So I pumiced and brushed and sprayed and bleached and trimmed and squirted and rubbed . . . and I discovered a terrifying fact. If I did all the things the magazines told me to do, I'd spend my entire life in the bathroom.

Caryl Rivers

Beauty is its own excuse for being.

Ralph Waldo Emerson

Because I have work I care about, it's possible that I may be less difficult to get along with when the double chins start to form.

Gloria Steinem

Beauty: the power by which a woman charms a lover and terrifies a husband.

Ambrose Bierce

Beauty's only skin-deep, but
ugly goes to the bone.

A. B. Evans

It was charming of God! I
never expected it! . . . That as
beauty vanishes the eyes grow
dimmer.

Mary Day Winn

The saying that beauty is but skin deep is a skin-deep saying.

Herbert Spencer

I'm a late bloomer. My mind and my experience have caught up to my body.

Raquel Welch

Beauty is the lover's gift.

Congreve

Vanity dies hard; in some obstinate cases it outlives the man.

Robert Louis Stevenson

It's not how old you are, it's
how hard you work at it.

Jonah Barrington

A man of fifty looks as old as
Santa Claus to a girl of twenty.

William Feather

Anyone can get old; all you
have to do is live long enough.
Groucho Marx

If youth be a defect, it is one
we outgrow only too soon.
James R. Lowell

Wrinkles are ditches that the
gods have dug for our tears.

Emile Augier

The worst form of ridicule to
which old people, once
charming, are susceptible, is to
forget that they are no longer
attractive.

La Rochefoucauld

Perhaps one has to be very old before one learns to be amused rather than shocked.

Pearl S. Buck

The years between fifty and seventy are the hardest. You are always being asked to do things, and yet you are not decrepit enough to turn them down.

T. S. Eliot

I do not say that I was ever
what is called "plain" but I
have the sort of face that bores
me when I see it on other
people.

Margot Asquith

Your body is the baggage you
must carry through life. The
more excess baggage, the
shorter the trip.

Arnold H. Glasgow

Not every woman in old slippers can manage to look like Cinderella.

Don Marquis

They say women and music should never be dated.

Oliver Goldsmith

If we do not know what we
are going to be, we cannot
know what we are: let us
recognize ourselves in this old
man or in that old woman.

Simone de Beauvoir

Most women are not so young
as they are painted.

Max Beerbohm

We are born with one face but, laughing or crying, wisely or unwisely, eventually we form our own.

Coco Chanel

Beauty and folly generally go hand in hand.

Baltasar Gracián

Beauty is altogether in the eye of the beholder.

Lew Wallace

By the time we hit fifty, we have learned our hardest lessons. We have found out that only a few things are really important. We have learned to take life seriously, but never ourselves.

Marie Dressler

I love everything that's old:
old friends, old times, old
manners, old books, old wine.

Oliver Goldsmith,
She Stoops to Conquer

Let the world know you as
you are, not as you think you
should be, because sooner or
later, if you are posing, you
will forget the pose, and then
where are you?

Fanny Brice

A very beautiful woman hardly ever leaves a clear-cut impression of features and shape in the memory: usually there remains only an aura of living color.

William Bolitho

When I go to the beauty parlor, I always use the emergency entrance. Sometimes I just go for an estimate.

Phyllis Diller

Do you know the difference between a beautiful woman and a charming one? A beauty is a woman you notice; a charmer is one who notices you.

Adlai E. Stevenson

It is only very rarely that age and beauty go hand in hand. The goddess of beauty, opportunist that she is, prefers to inhabit a young body.

Barbara Sichtermann

I have always felt that a
woman has the right to treat
the subject of her age with
ambiguity until, perhaps, she
passes into the realm of over
ninety. Then it is better she be
candid with herself and with
the world.

Helena Rubinstein

Better a bald head than no
head at all.

Seamus MacManus

There's no use being young
without being beautiful, and
no use being beautiful without
being young.

La Rochefoucauld

The years that a woman
subtracts from her age are not
lost. They are added to the
ages of other women.

Diane de Poitiers

The first half of our lives is
ruined by our parents and the
second half by our children.
Clarence Darrow

We are so vain that we even
care for the opinion of those
we don't care for.
Maria Von Ebner-Eschenbach

A man is as young as the woman he feels.

Anonymous

Everywhere one looks there is this glossy little animal, sometimes quite young and sometimes a little older, but always imagined, always pictured as The Girl.

C. W. Mills

We rely on the illusion of
beauty to convince ourselves
that true beauty is not so rare.

Barbara Sichtermann

Whatever pleases the heart
appears fair to the eye.

Sadi

The closing years of life are
like the end of a masquerade
party, when the masks are
dropped.

Arthur Schopenhauer

People who say you're just as
old as you feel are all wrong,
fortunately.

Russell Baker

So many beautiful women and
so little time.

John Barrymore

Though we travel the world
over to find the beautiful, we
must have it in us or find it
not.

Ralph Waldo Emerson

More precious in a woman is a virtuous heart than a face of beauty.

Kaibara Ekken

The perfection of outward loveliness is the soul shining through its crystalline covering.

Jane Porter

One evil in old age is that, as
your time is come, you think
every little illness the beginning
of the end. When a man
expects to be arrested, every
knock at the door is an alarm.

Sydney Smith

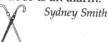

The body is most fully
developed from thirty to
thirty-five years of age, the
mind at about forty-nine.

Aristotle

A man may keep his nose to
the grindstone, but a woman
had better stop now and again
to powder hers.

Susan Brownmiller

Middle age is when your age
starts to show around your
middle.

Bob Hope

Time is a dressmaker special-
izing in alterations.

Faith Baldwin

Women are most fascinating
between the age of 35 and 40
after they have won a few
races and know how to pace
themselves. Since few women
ever pass 40, maximum
fascination can continue
indefinitely.

Christian Dior

Once upon a time, I was beautiful. My hair was thick and dark and glossy. My skin was smooth and soft as a ripe peach . . . my mouth was dark pink . . . My eyes were large and clear . . . Unfortunately, I was four years old at the time. It's been downhill ever since.

Geneen Roth

Self-love is subtler than the subtlest man in the world.

La Rochefoucauld

I have seen women of 70 and older in deep depression, almost a catatonic depression that nobody could seem to get them out of, until somebody thought of taking them to a beauty parlor.

Carlfred Broderick

You're never too old to become younger.

Mae West

When Gloria Steinem turned fifty . . . she updated her famous line from forty. She said, "This is what fifty looks like." With due apologies to the cult of midlife beauty, allow me two words: "Not necessarily."

Ellen Goodman

No wise man ever wished to be younger.

Jonathan Swift

The beauty that addresses itself to the eyes is only the spell of the moment; the eye of the body is not always that of the soul.

George Sand

I believe in hard work. It keeps the wrinkles out of the mind and the spirit. It helps to keep a woman young. It certainly keeps women alive.

Helena Rubinstein

Young and pretty women may delude themselves about the amount of abuse meted out to women, for as long as they are young and pretty, they escape most of it.

Germaine Greer

Charm is a glow within a woman that casts a most becoming light on others.

John Mason Brown

It is perhaps only in old age, certainly past fifty, that women can stop being female impersonators, can grasp the opportunity to reverse their most cherished principles of "femininity."

Carolyn Heilbrun

Old age is when the liver spots show through your gloves.

Phyllis Diller

Oh, grieve not, ladies, if at night
Ye wake to feel your
beauty going.
It was a web of frail delight,
Inconstant as an April
snowing.

Anna Hempstead Branch

Vanity is one of the major
forces of motivation in our
solar system.

Kate Gawf

Character contributes to beauty.
It fortifies a woman as her
youth fades. A mode of
conduct, a standard of courage,
discipline, fortitude and
integrity can do a great deal to
make a woman beautiful.

Jacqueline Bisset

As I grow to understand life
less and less, I learn to live it
more and more.

Jules Renard

The old believe everything;
the middle-aged suspect
everything; the young know
everything.

Oscar Wilde

She'll never admit it, but I
believe it is Mama.

Zsa Zsa Gabor,
when asked which of the
Gabors was the oldest

What is beautiful is good and who is good will soon also be beautiful.

Sappho

Here's my morning ritual. I open a sleepy eye, take one horrified look at my reflection in the mirror and then repeat with conviction: "I'm me and I'm wonderful. Because God doesn't make junk."

Erma Bombeck

Don't you pretend for a
minute as you look at me,
forty-three, fat, and looking
exactly my age, that I am not
as alive as you are and that I
do not suffer from the
category into which you are
forcing me.

Zoe Moss

Middle age: when you're
willing to get up and give
your seat to a lady—and can't.

Sammy Kaye

At age fifty, every [one] has the face he deserves.

George Orwell

I'm resigned to dying some day, but not to looking lousy for the next thirty years.

Edna Beilenson

Beauty is a short-lived reign.

Socrates

A thing of beauty is a joy
   forever:
Its loveliness increases; it will
   never
Pass into nothingness.

Keats,
Endymion

"Beauty is truth, truth beauty,"—
that is all
Ye know on earth, and all ye
need to know.

Keats,
Ode on a Grecian Urn

When you are young you
challenge your body. Now
your body challenges you.

Baryshnikov

The older I grow, the more I listen to people who don't say much.

Germain G. Glidden

Forty is fun because life has just begun. Age is mind over matter—as long as you don't mind, it don't matter.

Muhammad Ali,
prior to his last fight

The timing wasn't there and
the reflexes weren't there. I
could tell I was forty.

Muhammad Ali,
reflecting on his last fight

In fair bodies not only the
spring is pleasant, but also the
autumn.

Francis Bacon

One is vain by nature, modest by necessity.

Pierre Reverdy

A beautiful woman looking at her image in the mirror may very well believe the image is herself. An ugly woman knows it is not.

Simone Weil

It's a good thing that beauty is
only skin deep, or I'd be
rotten to the core.

Phyllis Diller

Youth is a blunder; manhood
a struggle; old age a regret.

Benjamin Disraeli

[People] can be cured of every folly but vanity.

Jean Jacques Rousseau

In every man's heart there is a secret nerve that answers to the vibrations of beauty.

Christopher Morley

The changes of my hair have reflected the changes of my life. And as I have fretted over my life, I have always fretted over my hair. . . . Of course I have never liked my hair. (What woman has?)

Erica Jong

Age is like love, it cannot be hid.

Thomas Dekker

From birth to age eighteen, a girl needs good parents. From eighteen to thirty-five, she needs good looks. From thirty-five to fifty-five, she needs a good personality. From fifty-five on, she needs good cash.

Sophie Tucker

I'm saving that rocker for the day when I feel as old as I really am.

Dwight D. Eisenhower

I realize that I like what my face has become. I could no longer conceive of it without its wrinkles. Anyone who is going to take me on is going to have to take on all of me, I'm afraid—with a full complement of years and the signs of their passage.

Elissa Melamed

It takes about ten years to get used to how old you are.

Unknown

Mirrors are our constant companions—and our companions are our constant mirrors.

Elissa Melamed

To me, fair friend, you never
 can be old
For as you were when first
 your eye I eyed,
Such seems your beauty still.

William Shakespeare

Middle aged people may be divided into three classes: those who are still young, those who have forgotten they were young, and those who were never young.

Lord Dawson,
British Royal Physician

I'm tired of all this nonsense about beauty being only skin-deep. That's deep enough. What do you want—an adorable pancreas?

Jean Kerr

You know you're getting old
when the candles cost more
than the cake.

Bob Hope

Women, when they are old
enough to have done with the
business of being women, and
can let loose their strength,
must be the most powerful
creatures in the world.

Isak Dinesen

Maybe I'm sick of the masquerade, I'm sick of pretending eternal youth ... sick of peering at the world through false eyelashes, so everything I see is mixed with a shadow of bought hairs ...

Germaine Greer

The best thing about getting old is that all those things you couldn't have when you were young you no longer want.

L. S. McCandless

A man's as old as he's feeling,
a woman as old as she looks.

Mortimer Collins

Every man desires to live long,
but no man would be old.

Jonathan Swift

Let us respect gray hairs,
especially our own.

J. P. Senn

I don't believe one grows
older. I think that what
happens early on in life is that
at a certain age one stands still
and stagnates.

T. S. Eliot

There are people who, like houses, are beautiful in dilapidation.

Logan Pearsall Smith

One should never make one's *début* with a scandal. One should reserve that to give an interest to one's old age.

Oscar Wilde

For the last third of life there remains only work. It alone is always stimulating, rejuvenating, exciting and satisfying.

Käthe Kollwitz

There are no ugly women, only lazy ones.

Helena Rubinstein

When the candles are out all
women are fair.

Plutarch

Time and trouble will tame an
advanced young woman, but
an advanced old woman is
uncontrollable by any earthly
force.

Dorothy Sayers

If we could see ourselves as
others see us, we probably
wouldn't take a second look.
Herbert V. Prochnow

Beauty doth varnish age.
William Shakespeare,
Love's Labour's Lost

A heart in love with beauty
never grows old.
Ancient Turkish Proverb

There is no excellent beauty
that hath not some strangeness
in the proportion.
Francis Bacon

The future is an opaque mirror. Anyone who tries to look into it sees nothing but the dim outlines of an old and worried face.

Jim Bishop

No Spring, nor Summer beauty
 hath such grace,
As I have seen in one
 Autumnal face.

John Donne

I love my past. I love my present. I'm not ashamed of what I've had, and I'm not sad because I have it no longer.

Colette

The body is not a permanent dwelling, but a sort of inn (with a brief sojourn at that) which is to be left behind when one perceives that one is a burden to the host.

Seneca

Every girl should use what
Mother Nature gave her
before Father Time takes it
away.

Laurence J. Peter

If the trousers do not attract
you, so much the worse; for
the moment I do not want to
attract you. I want to enjoy
myself as a human being.

Dorothy Sayers,
about women wearing pants

What is lovely never dies,
But passes into other loveliness.
Thomas Bailey Aldrich

Nature gives you the face you
have at twenty, but it's up to
you to merit the face you have
at fifty.

Coco Chanel

To gild refined gold, to
   paint the lily,
To throw a perfume on
   the violet,
To smooth the ice, or add
   another hue
Unto the rainbow, . . .
Is wasteful and ridiculous
   excess.

William Shakespeare,
   King John

Beauty when most unclothed
is clothed best.

Phineas Fletcher

The heart of the old is always
young in two things, in love
for the world and length of
hope.

Mohammed

It is not all bad, this getting old, ripening. After the fruit has got its growth it should juice up and mellow. God forbid I should live long enough to ferment and rot and fall to the ground in a squash.

Emily Carr

Beauty is but a flower,
Which wrinkles will devour.

Thomas Nashe

It is hard to admit the connection between a preoccupation with looking younger and a disgust with growing older. Yet the pleasure of being adored as a youthful beauty contributes to the pain of being rejected as an aging ugly. And the anxiety that is felt as the bloom of youth fades is one of the most destructive aspects of the beauty myth.

Rita Freedman

The longer I live, the more
beautiful life becomes.

Frank Lloyd Wright

Growing up means shaking
off the childish mask. Coming
of age with dignity means
looking as mature as we really
are and still seeing ourselves
as sensuous human beings.

Rita Freedman